How to
STOP
Drooling

MARSHALLA
SPEECH & LANGUAGE

Originally published as *Drooling: Guidelines and Activities,* © 1997

© 2014, 2009, 2006, 2004, 2002, 2001 by Pam Marshalla.
All rights reserved

Printed in United States

Marshalla Speech and Language
2305-C Ashland Street, PMB 318
Ashland, OR 97520

ISBN 978-0970706041

Dedication

This book is dedicated to Shanti, Ramana, and Namasté, my three beautiful daughters, who are teaching me more about children than I ever thought I needed to know.

Contents

Introduction

Drooling is a natural phenomenon in the development of all children. Babies and toddlers drool quite a bit each time they cut a new tooth. Drooling in young children is normal, and we often don't even notice it. But excessive drooling that occurs in children beyond the cute or "normal" age bothers us. We might call it *problematic* or *troublesome* drooling.

Troublesome drooling irritates adults and other children, and it can socially isolate the child who drools. Drooling is messy, it ruins things, and it can smell bad. It is an issue worth addressing.

This book will help you to reduce your child's drooling and eventually eliminate the problematic behavior. It is not a medical textbook, nor a workbook of activities; it is a resource of ideas, techniques, and methods you can use to help your child stop saliva from escaping the mouth.

The ideas in this book have evolved over twenty-five years of clinical work with children who drool to excess. From the perspective of a speech and language pathologist, it presents guidelines and activities that have proven useful in helping children to control, reduce, or eliminate problematic drooling behavior. It addresses the day-to-day "how to" of drooling management in a behavioral approach designed for parents and other caretakers, as well as for those who educate and treat children therapeutically.

The hope is that this work will prove beneficial to children who drool inappropriately and to excess, whether they are your own or your clients.

PLEASE NOTE: For simplicity, male gender pronouns (i.e., *he, him, his*) are used throughout to refer to the child who drools.

A Need for Information

Although excessive drooling is a very common phenomena in a wide variety of children and adults with speech and language disorders and related congenital or acquired neurological dysfunction, the process of saliva management has been ignored almost entirely in nearly every college and university research and training facility in the United States that has as its function the preparation of student speech and language pathologists or occupational and physical therapists. For the most part, those professionals enter their fields of special therapy services in schools, hospitals, and private practices without even the first idea of how to eliminate problematic drooling behavior. There is a crying need for research and therapy programs. This book has been written in the hopes that it will serve to stimulate those endeavors.

Chapter 1

Important Questions and Answers About Drooling

What Is Saliva?

Saliva is a naturally occurring substance that is produced by the salivary glands 24 hours a day, even when we are not eating. We swallow regularly throughout the day and night in order to remove excess saliva from the mouth and to keep the lips, chin, and face dry. When we let excess saliva seep or drip from the mouth, we drool.

Saliva has three important functions.

SALIVA IS IMPORTANT FOR

1. Speech—it keeps the inner mouth moist
2. Eating—it moistens food while eating
3. Digestion—it begins the digestive process

Speech

Humans are able to speak with ease because saliva keeps the inner mouth wet. Have you ever tried to speak with a dry mouth? Perhaps you had to give a speech or explain a difficult situation and your mouth became quite dry. You will recall that it was quite difficult to speak. Without saliva, the lips and tongue tend to move more laboriously and they stick to one another. That's why public speakers always have a glass of water at the podium to sip during their talks. Liquids and saliva keep the mouth moist for ease in speaking.

Eating

Humans are able to chew and swallow dry foods, such as crackers or cookies, because saliva mixes with the food during chewing. Again, have you ever tried to swallow dry food when your mouth was dry also? Do you recall the choking feeling you had when you tried to swallow that dry lump of food?

Food that is adequately moistened with saliva can be moved around easily during chewing, and the tongue can collect it efficiently in order to shape the food into a cohesive mass for swallowing. Moistened food also can be moved with the tongue from the mouth into the esophagus at the beginning of swallowing. Then the muscles of the esophagus can move food toward the stomach during the final part of swallowing.

Digestion

Saliva is the substance the human body uses to begin the digestive process. Saliva mixes with food in the mouth and begins to break down its sugars. Thus, food is already premixed with digestive juices by the time it gets to the stomach.

Isn't Drooling Normal in Childhood?

Yes! Drooling is quite normal in childhood during certain periods of time, especially throughout infancy and the toddler stages. These periods of excessive wetness usually coincide with the eruption of teeth. As teeth begin to poke through the skin, the brain is triggered that something is in the mouth and therefore more saliva needs to be produced. This excess saliva may help soothe the child's sore gums, but it also becomes unmanageable and is drooled.

When healthy and well-developed infants and toddlers are drooling in association with the eruption of teeth it should be of no concern to parents, educators, and medical personnel.

Why Does My Older Child Still Drool?

Children continue to drool beyond the age at which it is expected for four main reasons:

1. Saliva awareness—the child is not aware or doesn't care about saliva escaping the mouth
2. Swallow frequency—the child does not swallow often enough
3. Swallow efficiency—the child does not swallow effectively
4. Poor lip closure—the child keeps lips parted most of the time.

Saliva Awareness

The first reason children drool to excess is because they are not aware they are doing so. Saliva builds up in the mouth and they simply don't notice it. Children who do not notice that saliva is building up either can't perceive it or they ignore it. If they can't perceive it, it is because they either don't have the oral tactile and proprioceptive sensitivity that is needed to perceive the presence of saliva build-up, or they don't have the cognitive skills for this awareness—or both. Those children need help in sensing the presence of excessive saliva.

13

However, children with intact oral tactile and proprioceptive skills and who have high cognitive skills are not aware of their drooling because they have grown to ignore it. They have shut out the sensation of being wet much of the time.

The ability to shut out unwanted stimuli is a skill all humans possess. Without it we would be smothered by the uncountable stimuli that bombard us simultaneously throughout each and every day. We shut out sights, sounds, and thoughts in order to focus and to survive in our busy world. The older child with no cognitive or physical basis for this problem has begun to ignore his constant wetness. This child needs help in re-recognizing the excess saliva.

Intense concentration is also a trigger for occasional drooling in older children who have no disabling conditions. Drooling sometimes occurs when children concentrate very hard on a task such as writing. Intense concentration often causes children to let the facial muscles droop and the mouth to hang open. This type of occasional drooling should be of little or no concern to parents, educators, and medical therapists.

Swallow Frequency

The second reason older children drool to excess is because they do not swallow often enough. They may swallow less frequently because their awareness of saliva is poor, but the ultimate reason they drool is that they simply do not swallow often enough. Treatment is designed to help clients swallow more frequently and decrease their drooling.

Swallow Efficiency

The third reason older children drool to excess is because they swallow inefficiently. When a child has a weak swallow, or a swallow hampered by oral-motor or oral-sensitivity problems, he will swallow poorly and with limited efficiency. During eating, food particles will be pocketed in the space between the teeth and cheeks or between the teeth and lips. Food may remain pressed up against the roof of the mouth or all over the tongue.

When swallowing is inefficient, the mouth is not cleared of excess saliva during non-eating times. The saliva builds to the point of drooling. Even if the child is aware of the build-up, and even if he swallows frequently enough, the child will drool because his swallow is not well developed or well organized. Excessive saliva needs to be removed when the child swallows or drool will seep out.

Poor Lip Closure

The final reason children drool to excess is that they do not keep the lips closed during oral rest. Oral rest is that period of time when the mouth is not moving for speech or eating. During oral rest, the lips should remain gently together, forming a barrier that prevents the escape of saliva. The child who drools keeps his lips parted or is articulating them loosely. Treatment is directed toward increasing awareness and control of lip movements and establishing a closed-lip rest posture.

Can Drooling Be Eliminated?

Excess drooling can be controlled, reduced, and eliminated in many but not all cases. Success depends upon many factors, including the child's cognitive level, neuromuscular status, oral-tactile sensitivity, dental status, interest and willingness to participate in activities, alertness level, and oral muscle tone.

Obviously, children with little or no trouble in those areas should do quite well under a proficient management approach. Children with multiple confounding factors will take longer to change their behavior. Some clients, due to severe mental and physical conditions, will not succeed with the methods suggested here, and more invasive medical and surgical procedures must be considered. The appendix contains an excellent resource for such cases.

Why Use the Activities?

The activities and exercises described in this book will accomplish the following:

- *Heighten* the child's oral awareness and oral-tactile sensitivity
- *Increase* the child's swallowing frequency
- *Improve* the child's swallowing skill
- *Stimulate* and strengthen the child's closed-lip rest posture
- *Increase* the child's awareness of drooling
- *Encourage* the child to keep the face dry
- *Help* the child make a habit out of having a dry chin

Who Can Use the Activities?

The activities described in this book can be used by anyone who cares for, educates, or treats children who drool to excess. This includes parents, family and other daily caretakers, speech-language pathologists, occupational therapists, physical therapists, teachers, teacher aides, and student aides.

Ideally, representatives from several of those professions will work as a team with the parents to implement a successful drool-management program. The teamwork system is especially important for children with multiple disabilities.

Should the Activities Be Done Everyday?

Staying dry is a skill that can be learned like any other skill: by increasing awareness, practicing regularly, and maintaining those efforts over a period of time.

For example, consider the learning process in other venues. How many days per week should a child practice the piano, rehearse multiplication tables, or attend gymnastics classes in order to learn those skills? Obviously, regimented practice is beneficial to a certain point, after which the whole routine may become boring or too difficult.

New skills are learned by regular practice, but not by overkill. Adults who help children learn to stay dry have to use good judgment and common sense to discern how often and how long practicing these activities will benefit a particular child. One rule of thumb is to ensure regular activity in multiple environments over a period of time.

How Long Does Each Activity Take?

There are several different types of ideas, suggestions, and activities in this book. Some activities require time to be set aside, but none of them take more than 15 minutes to plan and execute. However, most of the procedures are simple ideas that can be shared and implemented during the course of everyday living, without designating special times.

How Long Does It Take to Stop Drooling?

The ability to stay dry cannot be taught overnight. It is learned in bits and pieces over a long period of time. For some children, this means weeks or months. For others, it means years. And, as was mentioned, some drooling problems do not go away.

It is helpful to think in terms of a six-month block. Six months seems to be enough time to get the child into the program, to practice skills, and to make some changes. If drooling is not reduced or eliminated in this length of time, a decision should be made whether or not to continue for another six-month period, or to take a break before working the activities again. Don't beat the problem into the ground. Be flexible and sensitive to the child's needs.

How Often Should I Do the Techniques?

Again, this depends on the child. For many children, the activities work best when they are concentrated over a period of time and success can be seen in a few weeks or months. For children with multiple compounding factors, these activities should be used on an intermittent basis over many years. Use your best judgment, and get together as a team to come to a joint decision about the length and duration of treatment.

Is There a Treatment Sequence?

This book begins with activities that require little control by the child and progresses up to those activities that require more skill by the child.

It is understood, however, that every child and every parent or therapist enters treatment with a history of other plans, knowledge of other techniques, and with prior success or failure in eliminating drooling. Therefore, readers should feel free to apply these ideas in a logical sequence that is most valuable to the child and the specific home, therapy environment, or school.

What Terms Should I Use?

For children of any age, the term *wetness* is a good one. Typically, *wetness* is a new word, whereas the terms *slobber, drool,* or *spit* may have been used by someone at home in a negative way, i.e., "Oh! He's slobbering all over my paper!"

To avoid negative associations with prior events and feelings that may have occurred with those familiar words, the term *wetness* is appropriate. Because most children have never heard this term used in this way before, it comes to treatment without prior associations. And, after all, wetness is what it is.

An older child may point out that the correct term is *drool* or *saliva*. In that case, acknowledge the term offered by the child and suggest using one or the other or both terms interchangeably. You might ask, "What should we call it when we work together?"

With some children, you may want to talk openly about all the names they have heard for saliva. A discussion in a loving and caring manner lets your child know that you are his friend when it comes to this topic.

Should I Follow Sanitary Procedures?

Yes! Whenever we touch a child around the face and mouth, and whenever we introduce a toy or other object to the mouth, we *must* follow sanitary procedures. This is easy to accomplish by following these few simple rules:

1. For hands-on procedures, a parent or other family member can simply wash with soap and water before touching the child, but professionals and other caregivers *must* wash

their hands with an antibacterial cleaner, or use an antibacterial lotion or wipe prior to touching the child.

2. Parents free of communicative diseases can work bare handed with their child, but professionals and other caregivers *must* wear sanitary rubber or vinyl gloves when touching the child. The gloves must be placed on the hands right after washing. Remove and discard gloves immediately after a single session. No gloves should be kept and used again at another time.

3. Parents and professionals *must* wash their hands again immediately after working with the child.

4. This program recommends the use of toothbrushes, washcloths, food, water and other liquids, ice cubes, spray bottles, lipstick, lipgloss, blow toys, straws, stuffed animals, and other common household objects to improve oral control. All toys, food, and other objects *must* be clean and safe. The objects *must* be designated for that child's use *only* and not shared from one child to another.

Are There Keys for Eliminating Drooling?

Here are five fundamental keys that will help to solve a child's drooling problem:

KEYS TO SUCCESS

1. *Increase* oral awareness
2. *Improve* swallowing frequency and efficiency
3. *Increase* the regularity of the closed-lip rest posture
4. *Motivate* the client for improvement
5. *Habituate* the new skills

The ideas in this book are organized into those five fundamental treatment areas. Each activity is explained so that a young child can understand what is being discussed. Adaptations must be made for children who will not understand the instructions, as well as for older children or adults who understand language at a much higher level.

Summary

Now, you have learned the following primary issues concerning drooling behavior:

1. Drooling is normal in early childhood, but it should come to an end at some time.
2. Drooling can be controlled or eliminated in many but not all cases.
3. Treatment involves increasing awareness of the oral mechanism, improving the frequency and efficiency of swallowing, improving lip control, and motivating and habituating new skills.
4. Eliminating the behavior of excessive drooling is a slow process that typically involves change over a period of time.

Chapter 2

Oral Awareness

*Learning About the Mouth
in Order to Stay Dry*

The term *oral awareness* refers to our conscious and unconscious awareness of sensations related to the mouth. Oral awareness allows us to perceive the build-up of saliva, the posture of the lips, and the process of swallowing.

When the conscious or unconscious mind senses that saliva has begun to increase in the mouth to a critical stage, an automatic swallowing response is triggered. If swallowing does not occur regularly, oral awareness allows us to perceive that drooling has occurred or is about to occur.

As described in the previous chapter, many children who drool to excess are not aware of the increasing amount of saliva building in the mouth and, when it seeps, they cannot feel it on their faces. Those children don't have enough oral sensory awareness and oral-tactile sensitivity to trigger the unconscious swallow response. Therefore, they are poor judges of when to swallow. The swallow response is not triggered often enough to prevent drooling in these children.

Whether or not they have normal or depressed levels of oral-tactile sensitivity, children with problematic drooling need to learn to become more aware of the tactile sensations inside and outside of their mouths. They also need to be aware of the amount of saliva accumulating in their mouths so that they can swallow before drooling occurs.

The following activities are designed to help a child become more aware of the mouth and the sensation of excessive saliva building up in the mouth and seeping out onto the lips and chin.

Teach the Concepts of *Wet* and *Dry*

For any drooling program to be a success, a child must understand the basic concepts of *wet* and *dry*. If not, the child won't understand the most fundamental aspect of the program. It is helpful to teach the concepts of wet and dry in other contexts before tackling the mouth. Here's what we can do.

When the child is playing in a bath, sink, pool, or bucket of water, make comments about how objects get wet. Over time, say:

- "You are so *wet.*"
- "Let's get your hair *wet.*"
- "Uh-oh. The floor is getting *wet.*"
- "*Wet, wet.* Your hands are all *wet.*"

Also use the term *dry* several times. For example, say:

- "Let's get you all *dry.*"
- "*Dry, dry, dry*—you love to be *dry.*"
- "Get the hair-dryer to *dry* your hair."
- "There! Now the toys are all *dry!*"
- "The towel made your hands *dry.*"

Take the time to show the child how to feel for wetness and dryness, and talk about the sensations. When things are dry, they feel smooth, soft, and silky. When things are wet, they feel rough, thick, or sticky. Towels glide across dry surfaces, whereas there is more friction as they drag across wet ones.

Other Times to Talk About Wet and Dry

- During diaper changing
- When a spill occurs
- While cleaning a countertop
- When playing in a sprinkler outside
- When transferring laundry from a washer to a dryer
- When watching birds in a bird bath
- When playing with finger paint
- When washing the car
- When blowing bubbles
- When blowing on wet things

There is virtually no end to the number of opportunities available in everyday-living routines to teach a child about wetness and dryness. Helping the child to understand wet and dry is often the first step to reducing drooling behavior.

Teach About a Wet and Dry Chin

The second step is to help the child discover that the chin is wet. Ask the child to feel his chin with his hands and describe it as wet or dry. Don't ask, "Are you wet or dry?" Say, "You are wet," or "You are dry." If the chin is already dry, say:

"Your chin is dry. That's great!"

If the chin is wet, give the child a dry washcloth or paper towel and ask him to wipe it. Say:

"Your chin is wet. Dry it off so it can be nice and dry."

Point out the wet and dry features as they apply to the child's chin. Establish the idea that adults like things dry, and they like the chin to be dry. Say, for example:

"Uh-oh, it's wet. We'd better dry your chin. It should be dry."

Learning about a wet and dry chin helps the child to become more aware of the mouth and the presence of saliva in it and on it. Usually, this is an early step in reducing drooling.

More Ideas for Teaching About Wet and Dry Chin

- Look in a mirror to see wetness and dryness
- Dry the chin carefully with a hair-dryer on a cool setting
- Get the chin wet with a wet washcloth, and then dry it with a dry washcloth
- Melt an ice cube by pressing it on and off the chin. Blow the chin dry. (Don't overdo this one; it might cause chapping.)

Teach Chewing

A child becomes more aware of the inside of his mouth when he practices chewing. Use food to discover chewing and to discover the inside of the mouth.

Select a time when the child is ready for a snack but is not so hungry that a full meal is needed. Make a snack of a small, dry food, such as fish crackers, oyster crackers, dry cereal pieces, small dry cookies, saltine crackers, or any other small dry-food snack. Prepare two glasses for drinking, one filled with cold water or juice and one empty. Don't use milk for this activity, because it is too thick and coats the inside of the mouth too much.

Arrange a mirror nearby. For example, face the child's chair to a wall mirror. Or sit at a table and place a freestanding mirror in front of him. A mirror about 1-x-2 feet is best so that you can see each other's faces but not too much else in the room.

Give the child one piece of food at a time and eat one yourself simultaneously. Don't hand over the entire snack to the child at once. While eating the piece of food, exaggerate your chewing motions by making them *big*. Chew with your mouth open and your lips spread so that the child can see your teeth and tongue.

While chewing, make sounds like "ahn-ahn-ahn" or "ahm-ahm-ahm" or "m-m-m". Many little children hum those as they chew. Making sound draws the child's attention to the act of chewing and forces the aroma of the food into the nose for smelling. It will help the child become aware of chewing and eating. Make comments about what you are doing, for example:

- "I am eating my cracker."
- "I am chewing my cookie."

Make comments about what the child is doing:

- "You are chewing your cracker."
- "I see your mouth opening and closing."

In these activities, the child's attention is drawn to the chewing process. This helps him become more aware of his mouth and the sensations in it.

Praise Wiping

When the chin is wet, it should be wiped dry. Some children do this automatically and some don't. Spontaneous wiping is a *good* sign. It indicates that the child already has achieved a certain level of oral awareness. If the child spontaneously wipes off his chin, notice this and give praise for the effort. Say:

"Hey! I saw you wipe your chin dry. That's great. We love dry chins."

If the child does not wipe yet, hand him a dry washcloth or soft paper towel and say:

"You need to wipe your chin dry. Please wipe it off. Get it all dry."

Keeping the chin dry is important. When the chin is constantly wet, children learn to accept it as normal. We want to teach the child a new dry sensation and that it feels good and is better.

Summary

In this chapter you have learned that, in order to begin the process of helping a child reduce or eliminate a drooling problem, you draw his attention to his mouth and its actions, making sure he understands the concepts of wet and dry.

Chapter 3

Swallowing

*Stay Dry by Improving Swallow
Frequency and Efficiency*

Swallowing is the process of using the tongue muscles to push food or liquid, including saliva, to the back of the mouth and into the throat. Then, swallowing continues with the neck muscles. They push the food or liquid down the throat, through the esophagus, and into the stomach. Swallowing regularly and skillfully prevents drooling.

All of us have saliva in our mouths at all times. The amount of saliva in the mouth constantly changes, depending upon atmospheric conditions like temperature and humidity, fluid levels in the body, and emotional or physical stresses in the body. The mouth is always producing a little bit of saliva, and, therefore, the amount of saliva in the mouth is always increasing slightly.

Sometimes the amount of saliva in the mouth increases a lot. For example, when we are hungry, our mouth "waters" at the thought or smell of a good meal. Throughout the day and during the night saliva increases naturally. Because of that, we have an *automatic* swallowing response. We don't have to think about swallowing our saliva; it occurs naturally.

Most of us are seldom aware of the swallowing process, because we just don't think about it. We eat and swallow every day, yet we hardly ever focus our attention on swallowing, except when one of the following occur:

- Something gets stuck in the throat
- We have a dry mouth or throat and cannot swallow easily
- We have a sore throat that causes swallowing to be uncomfortable

During those times, we think about swallowing because something is wrong. But during the course of everyday events, we rarely, if ever, think about swallowing.

Children with a problem of excessive drooling are as unaware of the swallowing process as the rest of us, even more so if they have poor oral awareness. Unless the child has a severe feeding problem, he is able to swallow, but probably is unaware that there is an action we call *swallowing*. We must draw the child's attention to the process of swallowing in order to eliminate drooling.

Swallowing

Swallowing is an important key to successful saliva management. Regular and successful swallowing prevents the amount of saliva in the mouth from getting out of control. Simply put, children with problematic drooling do not swallow often enough or with enough skill. They need to learn to swallow more often and with greater efficiency and strength.

Discover Your Own Swallow

In order to teach the child about swallowing, it is important that you first understand your own swallow. Prepare a glass of cold water for a learning activity. Cold water is easy to swallow and heightens the swallowing sensation.

In this activity, you will use your hands and fingers to feel the swallowing movements in your neck. To find the swallowing muscles of the neck, first use your fingers to locate your voice box or "Adam's apple." The voice box is hard and cartilaginous—like bone—and it moves up and down when we swallow. It is where our voice is produced, so it will vibrate when you say "ah."

Place your thumb on one side of the voice box and your fingertips on the other side. From there, move your fingers above the voice box and spread them widely on the neck to hold the muscles above the voice box right at the crook of the neck, where the neck turns under the chin. The muscles there will be soft and pliable.

Press your fingers into these muscles without causing pain, but hold firmly so you can feel the action of the muscles. These are the lower swallowing muscles.

Now, continue to hold your fingers there while you take a sip of water. Hold the water in your mouth for a few seconds, and then swallow. Notice how the muscles of your neck at the base of your tongue contract to pump the water down. You will feel an expanding movement of the muscles in there.

Repeat this several times until you are quite familiar with how the swallowing sensation feels in your fingers. You must be clear on what this feels like because it will be more difficult to feel it in the child's neck.

Children's muscles are smaller and weaker, and children with problematic drooling or low muscle tone usually have even less movement and strength in the swallowing muscles. Therefore, you must know what a good strong swallow feels like in order to be able to "read" the weak and immature swallow of the child with your hands.

Practice Makes Perfect

Consider feeling the swallow in another adult or child before you begin with your client. Once you can feel your own swallow and perhaps that of another child or adult, you are ready to work with the child.

Help the Child Discover Swallowing

Repeat the swallowing procedure described above with the child who drools. Poor one sip of ice-cold water into an empty paper cup and give it to him to swallow. Don't give him the full cup or he will take too many swallows at once and be unwilling to take any more. Give him only one sip at a time so that you can regulate how much he gets and so he will want to engage in the activity many times. (You can give him a full cup to drink all at once after you are through.) Let him hold the cup with the single swallow of water himself, and place your hand and fingers on his neck as you did your own. Make a preparatory comment, such as:

- "Do you know how to swallow? Let me feel it."
- "I wonder if you know how to swallow. Let me feel you swallow this water."
- "I will hold your neck to feel it."

When the child does swallow the sip, say:

"Oh! There it is! I felt it!"

As the child swallows, slightly press your fingers into the neck muscles right when they are at their deepest level of contraction. You may have difficulty determining when this is, but give yourself time and many trials to figure it out. The more rigorously you press into the swallowing muscles (without causing pain), the easier it will be to feel the swallow on the outside of the neck.

Next, show him how to use his own hand to feel his swallow. Take his hand in yours and place it appropriately on his neck above the voice box. Squeeze his fingers in to get him to squeeze in. Tell him, "Hold on tight." Then, as he swallows, say:

- "You're swallowing."
- "You're swallowing the water."
- "Do you feel the swallow?"

The pressure you apply to the muscles also helps the child feel the swallow from the inside. It gives him more information about what he is doing to swallow and increases his awareness of his own swallowing movements.

More Ways To Practice the Swallow

- Use a spray bottle to spray ice water into the mouth for swallowing.
- Use Popsicles, which melt quickly and provide a continuous stream of icy, good-tasting water to swallow. Challenge your child by saying, "Don't let it drip!"
- Let the child suck on an ice cube. As the ice melts, encourage the child to swallow the icy water and say, "Don't let it drip out!"
- Dip a Toothette in apple juice and let the juice drip into the mouth on the middle of the tongue. Say, "Swallow the drop."

- Use an eyedropper to place a few drops of ice water or cold applesauce into the mouth for swallowing. Place it in the middle of the tongue or on the side and say, "Swallow it."

The Clean Sweep

Another way to improve a child's oral awareness is to teach the *clean sweep*. The clean sweep is the action taken by the tongue after we swallow, clearing the mouth of all food particles. The tongue sweeps the mouth clear of food particles, and then we swallow again to evacuate or completely empty the mouth.

Many young children with problematic drooling do not use a clean sweep when eating, or they do it with limited success. They often swallow weakly, leaving quite a bit of food in the mouth. Food in little bits as well as big chunks can be stuck all around the mouth, both inside and outside. Food may be left on the roof of the mouth, between the cheeks and the teeth, under the tongue, on the lips, or even on the surface of the tongue itself.

The child probably is unaware of the leftover particles, or the child may be ignoring them. The child may not even care if the particles remain there. Leaving food particles in the mouth is a sign of limited oral awareness and limited oral control.

Our job is to help the child become aware of these leftover food pieces, to learn how to gather them with the tongue, and to learn to swallow them so the mouth will be truly empty. Learning these skills improves oral-tactile sensitivity and awareness.

Teaching the Clean Sweep

To teach the clean sweep, eat a dry snack together. While in the middle of chewing, open your mouth *wide* and look at it in the mirror. Say:

"Oh, yuck! I have lots of cracker all mashed up in my mouth. Do you?"

Encourage the child to look in his own mouth in the mirror. Then say:

"You do too! Yuck! We have to get rid of that. We have to make our mouths clean."

Then, with your mouth wide open, work your tongue conspicuously all around the mouth to clean all the surfaces. Make a big deal of it, with noises of effort and comments about how you are going to clean your mouth. For example:

- "That food is stuck all over the place."
- "I don't like that food stuck in there."
- "Look at the food on my tongue."
- "I have to get rid of it."
- "I'm going to get my mouth clean."
- "I have to get my mouth clean so I can have another cracker."
- "I can use my tongue to get all that food."

Sweep your mouth clean, swallow, and then look in the mirror again. Say, for example:

- "Look! My mouth is clean now."
- "I did it. I got all the pieces out."
- "My mouth is clean so I can have another cracker."

Then have another cracker together. As your child eats his cracker, ask:

"Did you swallow the whole thing?"

Encourage him to open his mouth and look in the mirror for any leftover bits. If you're sure there's still plenty of food in the mouth, try to catch him before he swallows much. Point out the mess in his mouth. Show him how to use his tongue to clear the teeth on the top and bottom, and from the molars on one side to the molars on the other side. Say, for example:

- "You have to swallow that cracker down."
- "Use your tongue. Get all the pieces."
- "You have to make that mouth clean to get another cracker."
- "Get that piece there."
- "Look at your teeth. See the cracker on there? Try to get all that off with your tongue."
- "Make your tongue go all around your mouth to get every piece."

Be sure to encourage the child to clean his mouth, or wait to give him another cracker until you are sure that the child has cleaned his mouth the best he can. Use a small swallow of water to completely flush the mouth clean of food bits, and talk about swallowing as described above. You are trying to get your child to clean the mouth as thoroughly as possible before getting the next cracker. The clean mouth is the goal; the next cracker is the reward for the clean mouth.

Continue until your child shows signs of getting full, bored, or disinterested. Try to quit just before these signs appear. You want to end the activity on a positive note, so don't push your child beyond their extent of interest.

For many children, the complete sweep of the mouth takes time to learn. It may be difficult to understand what you want at first, and it may be difficult to stretch the tongue that far. The child will get better with time and practice. Repeat this procedure several times over several days, weeks, or months until the child becomes proficient with the dry snacks and begins to incorporate the skill of complete evacuation in regular eating routines.

Learning to completely evacuate the mouth will help the child become aware of the presence of food particles in the mouth, and it will help him become more sensitive to changes in the mouth. In addition, the stretching exercises will help to increase tongue strength and the extent of tongue movement. Each of these skills will lead to better management of saliva.

Discover the Digestive Tract

To complete the child's knowledge of the eating sequence, after he swallows, ask the child, "Where did the water go?" Use your hands and fingers to touch the child's throat and "walk" your fingers down the neck to the stomach as you say:

"It went all the way down to your tummy."

You will help your child discover that his body can push food from the mouth down into the stomach by swallowing.

Teach the Dry Swallow

Many children with problematic drooling can swallow food or liquid easily, but they cannot swallow saliva alone. In other words, they cannot swallow on demand with only saliva in the mouth. Swallowing without the presence of food or drink in the mouth is called the *dry swallow*.

The dry swallow is not really dry. It's a swallow of whatever saliva has built up in the mouth. Sometimes there is a lot, and sometimes there is a little.

Children who cannot perform the dry swallow drool. These children need to be able to perform a dry swallow in order to manage their saliva.

It is difficult for anyone to perform a dry swallow many times in a row. Try it yourself: Try to swallow ten or fifteen times in a row without food or liquid. Notice how difficult it becomes after only a few swallows? Because of that, the dry swallow is taught with tiny amounts of water and practiced only once every few minutes. Here's what we do.

Engage the child in a 15-minute quiet activity of their choice and play with them. Select a puzzle, a coloring activity, Playdough, or another quiet, at-the-table activity. Follow the child's lead in the activity; you want him to have fun in the breaks between swallows.

During the activity and approximately every two minutes, pour a tiny sip of water into the empty cup and hand it to the child. Ask him to hold his neck as he swallows as described above. After he has swallowed two or three sips of water, challenge him to swallow without the water. Hold your fingers on his neck and say:

- "Can you swallow without any water?"
- "Let me feel. Ready? Swallow!"

Your child may swallow immediately. That is great. Praise the child for his performance. Say, for example:

> "You did it! You swallowed with no water in your mouth! That's great! I love it when you swallow."

If the child has difficulty swallowing without any liquid say:

> "Let's use a little water to help."

Give him a tiny sip of water and praise him for the excellent wet swallow. Alternate between wet and dry swallows until the child catches on and can perform the dry swallow. As described above, press into the neck muscles to encourage the dry swallow, and reward your child for any movement you feel in the neck muscles as he tries to swallow. A dropper with cold water works well in this activity.

The Difficult Dry Swallow

The dry swallow as described above is the most important skill the child will learn in this program, but it is one of the most difficult skills to learn. Many children take months to learn the dry swallow. Allow the child time to assimilate your directions and to learn this new skill.

Combine Wiping with Swallowing

Some children automatically wipe their faces dry when saliva has settled on the lip or chin. They usually use their hands, their shirtsleeve, or the front of their shirt to wipe it. It is important to realize that spontaneous wiping is a *good* sign. It shows the child is aware of the wetness and that it bothers him. We can use the child's automatic wiping response as a way to encourage more swallowing during the day.

Engage the child in a talk or activity. When you notice the child automatically wiping, say:

"Good job! You wiped your face dry. Now, swallow."

Use your hand to hold his neck as described above, and encourage him to swallow. Say:

"Every time you wipe, I want you to swallow."

This will not happen right away, but over time the child will begin to combine wiping with swallowing together. The wiping action will stimulate the child to swallow.

Watch for the Slurp!

Many children who drool will feel the presence of saliva on the lips and will slurp it up into the mouth. Slurping is another *good* sign. It indicates that the child is aware of the wetness and is attempting to manage it. Sometimes, when the saliva is just about ready to drop out of the mouth, parents will shout, "Johnny, swallow!" and the child will slurp the saliva back into the mouth.

Slurping is good because it brings saliva back into the mouth, but slurping is not swallowing, and often children who drool will slurp the saliva back in but will not swallow it. Therefore the saliva continues to stay in the mouth and will drip out again very soon.

When your child slurps, praise him and ask:

"Did you swallow it?"

Use the swallowing procedure to encourage him to swallow. Then say:

"When you suck it back in, swallow it too. Suck and swallow."

You are teaching the child to link slurping and swallowing together. When the slurp automatically causes the child to swallow, then saliva can be controlled better.

Stimulate Frequent Swallows with Cues

Select an auditory or visual signal you and others can use with him to cue him to swallow. I use both visual and auditory signals, especially sharp quick ones like a bell or the snap of a finger which can really get the child's attention at first but which can be faded or toned down over time.

Set up a table task play activity and, during the course of the activity, sound or signal the cue. Inform the child that whenever he hears or sees the signal, he is to wipe and swallow. Signal every two minutes or so, and make sure to follow through with the training. Increase or decrease the rate of stimulus presentation throughout the activity according to the child's needs, increasing it during times of intense training, and decreasing it in more relaxed play and when beginning to see results.

Teach Suction

To swallow efficiently and evacuate the mouth completely, a suctioning action must be performed *prior* to the final swallow. You can feel it when you swallow. Notice how you move your cheeks and lips around, pressing them against the teeth and suctioning inward to pull all the saliva toward the center of your mouth and onto the middle of the tongue for swallowing. While eating, suction is what ultimately clears the mouth of all food particles and liquid, and it's what readies the mouth for swallowing saliva the rest of the day.

The child who drools can be taught better suction by getting him to practice sucking on increasingly thick liquids through a straw, and by sucking pureed food off of other objects. Use straws of various diameters and lengths to vary the amount of sucking strength needed. Dip the bumpy ends of Nuk Massage Brushes into applesauce or yogurt and have the client suction it off.

Another very nice way to teach a child to suction is to use an eyedropper to deliver 1cc (less than ¼ teaspoon) of icy cold water or apple juice to the mouth. Place the tip of the dropper up against the underside of the top lip. Ask the child to grasp it with his lips. Tell him just to use the lips and don't let him bite on it. Now tell him to suck, and then squeeze the liquid out. Squeeze it hard and fast so it rather shoots into his mouth. This should set off the swallow reflex. Now you have a command ("*Suck*") that triggers him to suction and swallow. Gradually eliminate your squeezing action over time and ask the client to suck the liquid out without it. He should be able to do it if you have trained him well. Use this eyedropper method as a step before the dry swallow described above.

Over time, a child can become more adept at sucking liquids, and then that skill can be transferred to saliva. We might call it a *dry suction*, meaning that the child applies suction when no food or liquid is in the mouth, only saliva. Dry suction is encouraged during non-feeding times, and it is paired with wiping, slurping, and swallowing.

Teach Persistent Swallowing

The amount and frequency of drooling can vary tremendously from child to child. For example, some children drool the most while eating, while others drool only a little. Some drool more after a meal, during gross-motor activities, or while speaking. Others drool more in anticipation of a meal, during fine-motor activities, or while sitting quietly. Some children drool during oral-motor activities, and others drool less at that time.

For those reasons, we must be persistent in our observations of children and plan according to their individual needs. If oral-motor activities cause drooling to increase, we will have to cue the child to swallow more during that time. If drooling increases dramatically after a meal, the child must be monitored and cued to swallow at that time.

A successful drooling program demands fluidity and flexibility on the part of the family and all members of the service provider team. Goals and procedures should be selected to reflect the child's situation. Teaching a child to swallow more often and more effectively will be a part of every child's drooling-elimination program, but when, how, and under what situations the swallowing will be addressed should be determined by the specific drooling pattern of the child.

When Swallowing Is Absent

Some children who drool do so because they cannot swallow at all or because it is difficult to do so. Those children are not fed by mouth, but are fed through nasogastric (NG) or gastrointestinal (GI) tubes. Such children can benefit from the eating and swallowing methods described in this chapter, but, typically, these children are not ready to work only on saliva control.

For most people, saliva swallowing is a more difficult and a more refined skill than food swallowing because saliva is present all the time and not recognized by the child as unique in taste, temperature, bulk, texture, or smell. Once these children have accomplished oral-feeding skills, a program of saliva management can be initiated. In some cases, simultaneous work on both food and saliva swallowing can be coordinated.

Summary

In this chapter, you have learned how to teach the basic procedures for eating solids, including chewing, swallowing, sweeping the mouth clean, and suctioning. All of these discoveries can be coordinated into one 15-minute snack activity. By using water, juice, purees, and dry foods, you can teach a child about his mouth and increase the regularity and efficiency of his swallow.

Chapter 4

The Lips

Improving Lip and Facial Tone

Drooling can occur when the lips are parted but not when the lips are closed appropriately. Generally, children who drool have weaker lip strength and habitually part their lips, leaving their mouths open much of the time.

As you quietly read this book, notice your own lips. They should be "at rest," meaning that you are not eating, drinking, talking, or moving your mouth in any other way. This is the resting position of the lips. The lips should always be touching gently together when they are in resting position. This closed-lip rest posture works like a gate, helping to keep saliva in the mouth and prevent drooling.

From this resting position, swallow your saliva. If you have a normal, mature swallow, you will notice that your lips remain closed. The lips function to keep saliva in the mouth and enable the mouth to suction and accumulate the saliva. Whether you are swallowing saliva or another liquid, keeping the lips closed throughout the process helps to keep the contents inside the mouth. If the lips part, the contents can escape.

Children with troublesome drooling have problems keeping their lips closed during oral rest and during swallowing. These children often do not use their lips well, so they need to learn to keep their lips together. Good lip strength and successful lip closure during oral rest and swallowing helps to control, reduce, or even eliminate drooling.

Discover the Lips

You can employ many activities to help the child discover the lips and their actions. Children can:

- Make funny faces in the mirror. Accentuate lip positions, like smiling, frowning, kissing, and making the face of an animal or clown
- Put lipstick or lip gloss on the lips while looking in a mirror
- Press lipstick-colored lips onto tissue paper, paper napkins, or bath tissue to see the lip print
- Make "raspberries"—the sound made by pressing the lips together and blowing
- Blow on harmonicas, whistles, horns, and kazoos
- Blow bubbles
- Blow through straws
- Smack the lips
- Brush the lips with a dry toothbrush or a dry washcloth
- Use the fingers to stretch the lips outward on either side
- Pat a stuffed animal against the lips
- Suck on an ice cube (the lips must be closed to keep a melting ice cube in the mouth)

Throughout these activities, talk about the lips and reinforce their importance.

- "There are your lips!"
- "Hold the horn with your lips."
- "Can you make your lips do this?"
- "My lips are round."
- "My lips are stretched!"
- "Your lips are getting cold!"

Strengthen the Lips

Simple activities done on a regular basis can improve strength and control of the lips.

- Give kisses (full pucker) to a teddy bear 20 times in a row
- Press the lips together tightly while waiting for a traffic signal to turn green
- Blow up the cheeks and keep the lips closed
- Pretend to be a baby and say, "Ba-ba-ba-ba-ba" and "Ma-ma-ma-ma"
- Say "mommy" 10 times in a row
- Practice saying other words that begin with *m, b,* or *p*
- Hold a vibrator to the lips
- Press an electric toothbrush on the lips

Teach Lip Control

To get the child's lips together, use a small tool—straw, coffee stirrer, tongue depressor, swizzle stick, or another thin object. Then encourage the child to hold the lips together firmly for increasing lengths of time. Start with the following instructions:

"We're going to do a lip exercise. This is a [straw]. Hold it in your mouth for one minute. Don't use your teeth, and don't move your mouth around. Only use your lips. Don't let the straw move. I will tell you when you can take it out."

Make sure the child is holding the object only with the lips and is not using the teeth or the hands. It may be difficult for the child to hold the object without the lips becoming fatigued, but encourage him to hold it as long as possible. When the time is up, he can let go of the object. Repeat the activity at another time during the day.

Gradually increase the amount of time the child is required to hold the object. After he has achieved success, remove the straw and require him to keep the lips together all by themselves. The child can be involved in any quiet activity while practicing lip closure. Over time, plan for these activities to become more boisterous, so that the child has to work harder to keep the lips closed while handling more distractions.

Work Unconscious Control of the Lips

Ultimately, the lips should be closed while the child is engaged in other activities. Children who drool usually lose lip control while their mind is otherwise occupied. Use cues, stimulation, and reminders to keep the lips closed during other gross- and fine-motor activities. For example, touch between the lips with a tongue depressor intermittently while the child does a puzzle.

Massage the Face

Massage is a great way to tone up the face and lips. Periodic massage to the face can help the child become more aware of his lips and keep his lips closed during oral rest.

Place your fingertips on the child's cheekbones. Press gently but firmly and rotate slowly in circles.

Massage down to the middle of the cheeks and then down onto the chin. Return to the cheekbones and massage toward the upper lip. Continue around the mouth to the lower lip.

Massage is best when the child is reclining or lying down quietly. At home, select a time when you will not be disturbed, such as before bed, when taking a bath together, when grooming, when cuddling, or when watching TV together. During therapy, massage can be done while the child is reclined on a beanbag chair or on a mat.

Stabilize the Jaw

Children who habitually keep their mouths open do so because their lips are parted and because their jaws are allowed to sling too low. In the world of oral-motor therapy, this lowered jaw position is part of what is called *jaw instability*. Children who drool and who have low overall oral muscular tone almost always have the jaw slung low, the lips parted, and the mouth hanging somewhat open.

We can help a child support his upward jaw position and improve his closed-lip resting posture by activating and strengthening the *masseter muscles*. The masseters are those relatively large facial muscles situated on either side of the jawbone. They are the ones that pop out when we clench our teeth. The masseters are the primary muscles responsible for elevating the jaw.

In order to increase the activity of the masseters during speech, feeding, and oral rest, the child must discover and exercise those muscles. That will help elevate the jaw's overall habitual position and encourage a closed-mouth posture.

Ask the child to place his hands on your face and, with the fingertips, feel your masseters at the point where they contract the most while clenching.

Alternate between clenching and relaxing so the child can feel the muscles bulge out and pull back in. Ask the child:

"Do you feel my muscles popping out?"

Make sure the client understands that you are not talking about dislocating the jaw. "Popping" refers to the contraction of the masseter muscles during clenching—the muscles bulge out during contraction and retreat inward during relaxation.

Then encourage the child to clench his own jaw while you feel his masseters. Put a little bit of fingertip pressure on the muscle bellies as he clenches so he gets an idea of where to make the action occur. Children with low oral tone and related habitual open-mouth posture will demonstrate limited ability in clenching. At first, you may not feel any muscle action whatsoever. With time and repeated attempts, however, the child will learn to clench with greater strength and "pop out" his masseters.

As the masseters increase in strength, you will notice that the child will begin to hold the jaw in a more elevated position during oral rest and speech, and he will begin to show greater strength in biting and chewing. Better lip closure will ensue, and tongue movement will improve. Better lip and tongue movements set the stage for efficient saliva swallowing and drooling management.

Summary

In this chapter, you have learned how to increase the child's awareness and control of his facial muscles, and how to encourage a closed-lip rest posture. The goal has been to teach the child that keeping the mouth closed will help prevent drooling.

Chapter 5

Motivation and Habituation

More Ideas to Help Your Child Stay Dry

The final stage of a successful program to reduce or eliminate drooling involves *motivating* the child to change his behavior, and *habituating* the newly learned skills over time.

For children who drool, staying motivated to keep their chins dry can be a problem. Their mouths or chin are wet so much of the time that they tend to ignore and accept it. It feels normal and right to be wet.

Children with problematic drooling must become aware that they are wet on the face. They need to learn that a dry face is preferable, and they need to be motivated without shame, guilt, or scolding. This chapter discusses how to talk to your child about the situation in order to promote positive change.

Brainwash Your Way to Success

Once you decide to help a child learn to eliminate drooling, everything you say in front of him about this topic, and everything other people say, will teach him how well he is doing in the program. Everyday comments about drooling become firmly ingrained in the child's conscious and unconscious beliefs about himself.

Withhold Negative Comments

Some statements make children feel bad about drooling and about themselves. They send the message that the children are helpless to change. Negative statements make children resentful of the adults who say them, and children who receive negative statements are less willing to participate in activities and less interested in pleasing adults with progress. Do any of the following sound familiar?

- "Can't you ever stay dry?!"
- "I am sick of this slobber!"
- "You'd better learn to swallow, or else!"
- "That is disgusting!"

Take time to pay attention to how you and others talk about the child's drooling. Do you make fun of him? Do you express disgust at the drooling behavior? Do you chastise, ridicule, or belittle the child for it? Do you treat the child as if change is impossible?

Make Positive Comments to the Child

Statements we make can help children feel good about learning to stay dry. These statements help children build positive attitudes about the program and about themselves as they learn to stay dry:

- "You're getting so big! I saw you wipe the wetness off your chin."
- "You're dry. Yeah!"
- "Oh no. Wet again? Dry it off."

- "Oh, I like how well you swallow."
- "I can't believe you swallowed the whole thing. I am so impressed!"
- "Dry is what we like, and dry is what you are."
- "Do you want to talk to Grandma on the phone? Here, wipe your face dry so you'll be all ready. There you go. You're dry now! Here's the phone. Say, 'Hi.'"

Praise Dryness

Behavioral child psychologists discovered long ago that behaviors that are noticed and rewarded tend to increase in frequency, and those behaviors that are not noticed or rewarded tend to decrease in frequency. In other words, the more we pay attention to something the child does, the more the child will do it. If we only talk about their drooling and we never mention the times when their faces are dry, children will gain awareness of wetness but will learn little about attaining dryness.

In this regard, make sure to pay attention to a child's dry face. During the course of the day, notice when your child has periods of dryness. Make affirming comment, such as:

- "Wow! Your face is completely dry right now!"
- "You know what? I watched you during that show and your face was dry the entire time."
- "Remember when we talked about a dry chin? Well, your chin is dry right now and I want you to know that I like that."
- "Oh, this is really good! You are completely dry! We walked all the way to school and your chin in still dry. That is very good."

Make Positive Comments to Others

Statements made to others about a child's drooling can give the child hope and make him feel as if he were changing right in front of your very eyes. It also makes your child feel good that the adults who are important to him are proud of him.

- "He's staying dry more of the time. I am so proud of him."
- "He did all the lip exercises today. I think he's going to make it!"
- "Yes, he's still drooling, but that is changing. He's going to be dry pretty soon."
- "I watched him during a movie today, and he was dry through the first half. When he got wet, I gave him a washcloth and he wiped it off all by himself."
- "Sammy kept his lips closed for 15 minutes today while we rode to the dentist."
- "Sammy's lips are getting stronger. He can hold them closed even when we try to open them."
- "Sammy was sucking on ice today—weren't you, Sammy? It was really cold! Tell Daddy what you did with that ice."

Habituation

Any habit is hard to change, and children who drool to excess face a difficult challenge. Changing the habit takes time, determination, motivation, commitment, and will. It also takes rehearsal of the new skill. This fifth and final key to successful saliva management is called *habituation*—making a habit. These activities will help make a dry chin a strong new habit.

Make Up a Song

Singing about something helps us to remember it. For example, advertisers use songs all the time to promote their products by causing us to feel more emotional about them. Then, we are more likely to remember those products and buy them.

Songs can be used in a drooling program to help make activities fun and to help drive the concepts into the child's conscious mind. Songs can describe a certain part of the program and they can summarize the goals to be met. They also can praise the child for how well he is doing. You can borrow an old familiar song or you can make one up on your own. Kids don't seem to care how good or bad our voices are, so loosen up and let it out!

Here are a few lyrics to get you going. You will have to come up with your own tunes.

> We love to be dry.
> We love to be dry.
> We dry our faces
> 'Cause we love to be dry!

> Emily is growing.
> She's not very shy.
> She's almost six and
> She's learning to be dry!

> Swallow, swallow, swallow.
> Food goes down my throat!
> Swallow, swallow, swallow,
> Swallow like a goat!

> A-B-C,
> 1-2-3,
> Wipe-wipe, swallow-swallow,
> Look at me!

Make a Habit out of Staying Dry

It is easier for a child to stay dry when he is engaged in songs and activities designed to focus on these things. But it is harder to do so when other interests become a distraction. To create the new habit of staying dry, we have to help the child remember to check his wetness or dryness periodically while he is engaged in other activities.

Select a 15-minute activity that your child likes. Set a timer to ring every two minutes. When the timer rings, say, "Check your chin, see if it's wet or dry." Encourage the child to touch his chin, and praise him if it's dry. If it's wet, ask him to wipe it off. As the activity progresses, fade your instructions out. For example, when the timer rings, look to the child with wide eyes and expectation but do not tell him what to do. If he doesn't wipe right away, say, "The timer went off. What should you do?" Reward the child for remembering to wipe. Over time, give fewer reminders and change the timer to ring less often.

Large-motor activities also can be used for this activity, but make sure the child stops his activity completely when he checks his chin. Say,

> "Danny, stop! Come here. It's time to check your chin . . . OK, now you can go back and play."

Use Wristbands and Wipe-Wipe-Swallow

Many children drool almost continuously and will need some way to wipe the drool away without using their hands or a shirtsleeve. Athletic wristbands or "sweat bands" work well. Place one athletic band on each wrist. Train the child to follow a three-step procedure:

A) Wipe the *left* side of the mouth with the *right* wristband

B) Wipe the *right* side of the mouth with the *left* wristband

C) Swallow

It is important that all three steps be used together in the sequence. First, if the child wipes only one side, that side may get stronger and drool less while the other side stays weak and lets saliva escape. Secondly, rehearsing all three steps each time trains the child to swallow more often. Over time, the presence of the wristbands themselves will begin to trigger the swallow. Wristbands need to be worn for one day and then laundered.

Some children will benefit from naming this swallowing procedure the "ABC Swallow." *A* is the first wipe, *B* is the second wipe, and *C* is the swallow. By naming this procedure, anyone in the child's home or at school can cue him to swallow by saying "ABC" or simply "A." That can become a secret signal to wipe and swallow.

Use Reward Systems

Many families use reward systems to increase or decrease selected behaviors in their children. For example, some families keep a "Star Chart," which records the times when the child does household chores like making the bed, keeping the bedroom picked up, or putting the dishes away. When a predetermined number of stars have been achieved, children earn an enticing reward, such as a movie rental, visiting the zoo, taking a bike ride together, or ice cream.

Reward systems can be used with any programs or activities that help reduce, control, or eliminate problematic drooling behavior.

Summary

In this chapter, you have learned techniques that will motivate your child to practice the skills he needs to stay dry and habituate the process.

Summary

Sometimes the habit of drooling to excess can be reduced or eliminated, but other times it can only be controlled. In either case, problematic drooling can and should be addressed by parents, educators, and therapists. Most children will progress if given time, encouragement, and good remediation procedures.

I hope that this little book has stimulated you into creating drooling elimination programs that will help your clients stay dry. I also hope that this book will encourage more effort on the part of university training programs to investigate the drooling problems of individuals with speech and language problems, and in training student therapists to plan for and manage saliva problems in their future client caseloads.

Additional Information

Breathing Problems and Drooling

Upper airway problems, such as recurring allergies, sinus infections, swollen adenoid or tonsils, or structural problems in the nose, can contribute to a problem with drooling. When children cannot breath through the nose easily and regularly, they often develop a habit of keeping the mouth open to breathe. As mentioned earlier, when the lips are constantly parted, drooling can occur.

Discuss these problems with the child's physician to discover how upper airway problems are interrelated with the child's drooling problem. In some cases, medical or surgical intervention strategies will be discussed and plans determined. The plan must be shared with all of the child's therapists and educators so that everyone involved with the child will continue to work toward the same goals.

Drooling with Multiple Disabilities

A child with multiple disabilities is at considerable risk for drooling. Their physical health, muscle tone differences, attention deficits, depressed or elevated levels of oral-tactile sensitivity, feeding problems, and neurological state contribute to problematic drooling that can continue for life.

Success in the reduction, management, or elimination of drooling in children with multiple physical and mental disabilities can be achieved when the activities offered in this book are used in conjunction with good programs that develop alertness, attention, comprehension, sensory awareness, feeding skills, and movement abilities. When more pervasive disabilities are a part of the drooling syndrome, a broader path of remediation is needed and a longer timeframe for change is required.

An Excellent Resource

An outstanding source of information about the control of drooling can be found in *A Practical Approach to Saliva Control* by Hilary Johnson and Amanda Scott (1999). It discusses drooling remediation from a medical and surgical perspective, and presents therapy strategies for occupational therapy, physical therapy, and speech-language pathology, as well as surgical and pharmaceutical options. It is available through:

Communication Skill Builders
555 Academic Court
San Antonio, TX 78204-2498

Telephone: 1-800-228-0752
Fax: 1-800-232-1223

Additional Resources by Pam Marshalla

How to Stop Thumbsucking
And Other Oral Habits

Vowel Practice Pictures
375 Drawings for Vowel Practive

Frontal Lisp, Lateral Lisp
Articulation and Oral-Motor Procedures for Disgnosis and Treatment

Successful R Therapy
Fixing the Hardest Sound in the World

Carryover Techniques
In Articulation and Phonological Therapy

Oral Motor Techniques
In Articulation and Phonological Theapy

Becoming Verbal With Childhool Apraxia
New Insights on Piaget for Today's Therapy

Apraxia Uncovered
The Seven Stages of Phoneme Development

Do You Like Pie? - CD
Songs for Phonemes, Syllables, and Words

The Four Stages of Imitation - DVD
Facilitating Sound and Word Production in Young Children Who are Non-Verbal